A Flower Triptych

Daffodils 3

The Narcissus 19

The Flowers 29

Celebrating the Use of Flower Imagery in *A Flower Triptych*
an introduction by Leslie Schroerlucke, composer

A Flower Triptych celebrates the poetic use of flower imagery with choral settings of three English poems. The idea for the series was inspired by William Blake, who in his "Auguries of Innocence," wrote,

> To see a World in a Grain of Sand
> And a Heaven in a Wild Flower,
> Hold Infinity in the palm of your hand
> And Eternity in an hour.

William Wordsworth echoes similar pious sentiments towards nature in several of his poems. In "Daffodils," communion with a field of blooming flowers dissipates his loneliness and moves him to a blissful state.

John Keats refers to a "lonely, forlorn, flower reflected in a glassy pool" that symbolizes the ancient story of Narcissus, who failed to recognize Echo's love for him because of his obsession with his own reflection. "The Narcissus" cites the seventh stanza from Keats's 1817 poem, "Places of Nestling Green for Poets Made," subtitled "The Story of Rimini," dedicated to the Poet Leigh Hunt.

Robert Louis Stevenson's "The Flowers" transports the speaker back to the innocence of childhood and certainty in the existence of fairies. I have a great reverence for nature and find my own interaction with it both grounding and transcendental. My many retreats to nature provide solace, especially in challenging times. I believe that nature can provide many epiphanies if we only take time to observe and reflect.

978194838062-1 • International Standard Book Number, paperback
978194838063-8 • International Standard Book Number, ebook

Music, introduction, performance notes, acknowledgments, and composer biography © 2022 by Leslie Schroerlucke. Contact the publisher at marcia2gagliardi@gmail.com for pdf files free of charge with your receipt of purchase of the physical copy and a license to make photocopies of the copyrighted songs.

Cover photograph © 2022 by Eva Elijas via download from Pexels.

Copy edited by Lynn Boudreau.

All rights reserved. With the exception of short excerpts in a review or critical article, no part of this publication may be re-produced by any means, including information storage and retrieval or photocopying equipment, without written permission of the publisher, Haley's.

Words by William Wordsworth, John Keats, and Robert Louis Stevenson found in the public domain.

Performance Notes for *A Flower Triptych*
by Leslie Schroerlucke, composer

"Daffodils" should be sung with a pondering, reflective quality. The addition of male parts throughout the song needs to communicate increasing joy and elation. "The Narcissus" is a reflective and stately ode to unrequited love and missed opportunity. It should be sung slowly and expressively. "The Flowers" is a lighthearted song that expresses memories of childlike innocence, hope, and a belief in the fantastic. Aim for a joyful and celestial vocal quality.

The songs are intended to be performed as a set in the order presented. However, feel free to perform each on its own. All are scored for SATB, but adjustments are encouraged for younger or less experienced choirs. "The Narcissus" is intended to be performed a capella with piano accompaniment for rehearsal only, but use your judgment to make adjustments that will work with your ensemble.

I hope that you and your group will enjoy working on this music together! With the purchase of this music, each director also purchases the rights to create performance videos and permission to stream or upload them to the internet.

Acknowledgments from the Composer

I thank Dr. David Rentz for his choral advice and support and Robert Davis and the talented Ayala High School Choir for providing the first readings of *A Flower Triptych*. I thank Rich Langham and the Diamond Bar High School Choir for the first performance. Many thanks to the indomitable Marcia Gagliardi for her unwavering encouragement to publish my songs.

About the Composer

Leslie Schroerlucke earned a bachelor of music degree and performer's certificate in clarinet performance from Eastman School of Music, Rochester, New York; a master's of music degree in clarinet performance from Florida State University, and a master's degree in music education from Boston University. She enjoys a dual career as an orchestral clarinetist and a band director with Walnut Valley Unified School District in Diamond Bar, California. She serves on the faculty of the University of California at Riverside and Chaffey College in Rancho Cucamonga, California.

A native of central Massachusetts, Leslie resides in southern California where she is an active performer in several musical communities. *A Flower Triptych* is her first published work.

For more information, tracks, and pdf purchase, visit flower triptych.com.

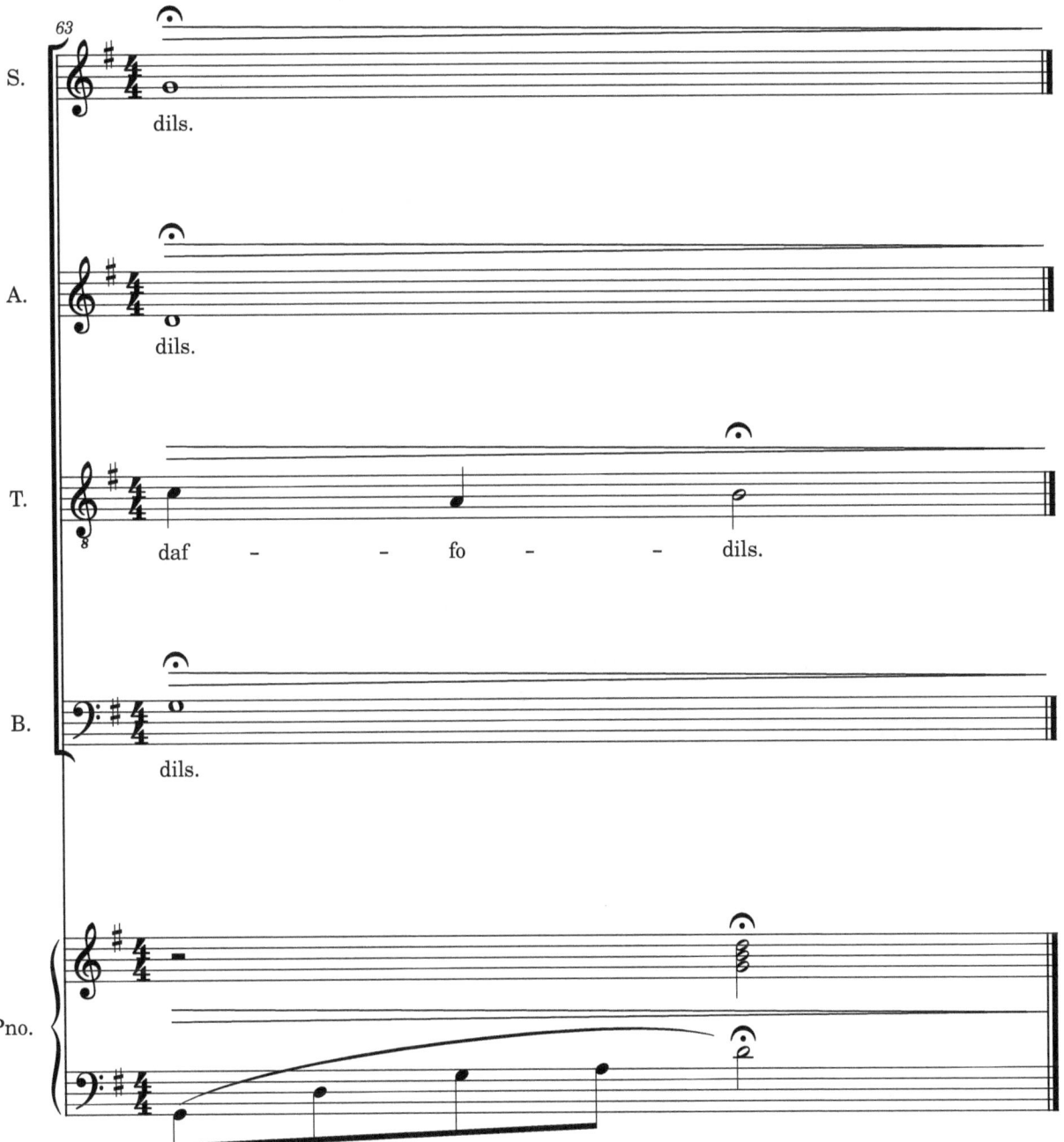

The Narcissus

lyrics from the poem "Places of Nestling Green" by John Keats, 1795-1821

Music by Leslie Schroerlucke

The Flowers

Lyrics by Robert Louis Stevenson
Music by Leslie Schroerlucke

29

www.ingramcontent.com/pod-product-compliance
Lightning Source LLC
Chambersburg PA
CBHW080803020526
44114CB00046B/2875